100

POWERFUL QUOTES TO UNLOCK THE MINDSET OF UNSIGNED ARTISTS

WRITTEN & HOSTED BY

DJ FRANK WHYTE

THIS BOOK IS DEDICATED TO:

(Rest In Peace)
(MOTHER & FATHER)
(PATRICIA BATTLES & FRANKLIN JONES)

MARY BRIDGES
KEVIN BRIDGES
JAMES BRIDGES
CRYSTAL BATTLES
CALVIN COOLEY
ANETTE SIMPSON
(BIG)CHARLES KEENE
(LITTLE)CHARLES KEENE
LORENZO KEENE
YASMIN CRYSTAL GRANT
NIASHA TIFFANY GRANT
JAYVON GRANT AKA JAY JAY
RON DEAN

ACKNOWLEDGMENTS

HOW DOES AN AUTHOR LIKE ME SAY THANK YOU WHEN THERE CAN BE SO MANY PEOPLE TO THANK BUT OBVIOUSLY, IT IS ONLY GOD AND MY MENTOR AND EDITOR, KEITH WILLIAMS, DAWN ELLISON, CEO OF CODE 31 MEDIA, J HATCH, CEO OF CREATIVE SPACE, WILLSTYLZNYC, CEO OF MAJOR RECORD LABEL

THIS BOOK BECAME A REALITY BY USING THE WORD, *MANIFESTATION*. IT TAUGHT ME THE TRUE MEANING ALONG THE WAY WITH ENERGY, VIBRATION AS AN AUTHOR BUT BY LISTENING TO A FRIEND OF MINE, DAWN MERRICK, WHO SAID, "ANYTHING IS POSSIBLE WHEN IT COMES TO MANIFESTATION."

INTRODUCTION

ATTENTION ATTENTION!

UNSIGNED ARTIST, BATTLE RAPPERS,
AUTHORS, MODELS, MUSIC PRODUCERS
AND ENTREPRENEURS!

COME BE THE NEXT V.I.P GUEST ON
UNSYNEDHEATTPODCAST CLUB SHOW
HOSTED BY DJ FRANK WHYTE. WE FEATURE
TALENT ON THE RISE MONTHLY WHO HAVE
REAL LIFE STORIES TO TELL US AND THE
WORLD. WE WILL TALK ABOUT UPDATES
AND THE LATEST NEWS, PRODUCTS,
EVENTS, AND NEW PROJECTS ON THE WAY
FROM MAJOR ARTISTS, UNSIGNED ARTISTS,
MUSIC PRODUCERS, MODELS AND AUTHORS.
WE WOULD LOVE TO HAVE YOU ON AN
EPISODE SO BEFORE ALL THE SLOTS ARE
FILLED UP, LOCK IN YOUR V.I.P SEAT.
LET US KNOW IF WISH TO PROCEED.
PLEASE TELL A FRIEND.

CONTACT US

EMAIL
UNSYNEDHEATTPUBLISINGWORLD@GMAIL.
COM

EMAIL
FRANKLIN.BRIDGES77@GMAIL.COM

CONTACT 646 404 6755

1 - ALWAYS REMEMBER AS A NEW ARTIST, YOUR SUCCESS WILL BE TRIED TO THE COMPANY THAT YOU KEEP AS YOU BUILD YOUR MUSIC CAREER IN TIME. SO ALWAYS LOOK TO YOUR LEFT AND RIGHT WHEN IT COMES TO HAVING FRIENDS OR A TEAM IN THIS MUSIC INDUSTRY BECAUSE CAN RUN INTO A LOT OF FAKE PEOPLE THAT DON'T HAVE YOUR BACK BUT REMEMBER GOD GOT YOUR BACK.

2 - THE MUSIC INDUSTRY IS A GRIND. IT'S VERY GRITTY TO GET TO THE TOP. YOU GOT TO GO THROUGH THE UNDERGROUND LIKE BARS, SMALL ROOMS, CLUBS, STRIP CLUBS, OPEN MIC'S SHOWCASES OR CREATE YOUR OWN OPEN MIC OR SHOWCASE. THAT WAY YOU CAN BE YOUR OWN OPENING ACT THAT YOUR FANS SEE FIRST.

3 - IF ANY RECORD LABELS ARE LOOKING TO SIGN YOU, DON'T LOOK FOR THE MOST MONEY. LOOK FOR THE MOST OPPORTUNITIES THEY CAN GIVE YOU BECAUSE YOU ARE BUILDING WEALTH FOR YOUR FAMILY AND KIDS. THE MORE OPPORTUNITIES THAT YOU CREATE WILL OPEN UP OTHER DOORS WITHOUT THEM BEING LOCKED.

4 - ALWAYS STAY FAR AWAY FROM PEOPLE WHO HAVE NO AMBITIONS OR DREAMS IN LIFE, BECAUSE AT THE END OF THE DAY GOD WILL POINT THEM OUT FOR YOU, BUT IT'S GOING TO BE UP TO YOU TO USE YOUR THIRD EYE TO SEE THEM AS WELL. SO ALWAYS MAKE GOD YOUR BEST FRIEND WITH YOUR OWN DREAMS AND AMBITIONS.

5 - LIFE IS TOO SHORT FOR YOU TO EVEN WASTE A DAY NOT TRYING TO ACHIEVE YOUR DREAMS. SO START TAKING CONTROL OF YOUR OWN TIME AND GOD WILL DO THE REST AS YOU CONTINUE TO BE THAT STAR IN THE SKY WITH A HUSTLE THAT COSTS MORE THAN WHEN THE RECORD LABELS GIVES YOU ADVANCE MONEY. SO GRIND, GRIND, HUSTLE, HUSTLE, WIN, WIN.

6 - STAY FOCUSED AND DON'T LET ANY TYPE OF DISTRACTION OR INSECURITY STOP YOU FROM BRINGING YOUR DREAMS TO LIFE IN THIS CRAZY WORLD YOU LIVE IN AS A NEW ARTIST BECAUSE YOUR DREAMS ARE VERY POWERFUL. YOU CAN CONTROL THEM IF YOU PUT YOUR MIND AND ACTION TO THE TEST. IF YOU CAN ACHIEVE 60 % OF YOUR GOALS, IT MEANS YOU ARE FOCUSED. YOU JUST NEED 40% TO ADD UP TO 100%.

7 - AWAY BE THAT ARTIST OF YOUR WORD BECAUSE IF YOU SAY YOU ARE GOING TO DO SOMETHING, DO IT. THAT WAY YOUR FANS WILL START RESPECTING YOU EVERY TIME THEY SEE YOU ON STAGE OR WHEN THEY MEET AND GREET YOU BACKSTAGE AT A SHOW. THEN YOU WILL START TO SEE THE DIFFERENCE ON HOW YOUR WORDS AND YOUR RESPECT WILL GROW OVER TIME.

8 - AS AN UP AND COMING ARTIST, YOU SHOULD ALWAYS NETWORK WITH EVERYBODY AROUND YOU WHEN YOU PERFORM AT SHOWCASES, OPEN MIC'S OR ANY OTHER EVENTS. AND THAT GOES FOR SECURITY, JANITORS, THE CLUB PROMOTORS, THE WAITRESSES AND WAITERS, MANAGERS, COOKS, DISH WASHERS, ETC. THE LIST GOES ON AND ON BECAUSE YOU DON'T KNOW WHO THEY KNOW AND THESE PEOPLE CAN CHANGE YOUR LIFE.

9 - IF YOUR FRIENDS AND FAMILY DON'T BELIEVE IN YOU FROM THE BEGINNING, LET THEM KEEP THAT SAME ENERGY AS NONBELIEVERS BUT WHEN YOU MAKE IT AND BLOW UP, THAT'S WHEN PEOPLE START ACTING LIKE THEY BELIEVED IN YOU FROM THE BEGINNING. THEY DIDN'T UNDERSTAND THE POWER THAT YOU ALWAYS HAD INSIDE YOU THAT WAS GOING TO IMPACT THE WORLD AS THEY BECOME FANS OF YOUR MUSIC AND DREAMS.

10 - ALWAYS BE AWARE OF THE PEOPLE AROUND YOU BECAUSE YOU NEVER KNOW WHO THEY ARE UNTIL THEY SEE HOW MUCH MONEY YOU ARE MAKING OR WHAT THEY CAN GET FROM YOU SO YOU MUST UNDERSTAND THAT EVERYBODY IS NOT YOUR FRIEND AND EVERYBODY IS NOT YOUR FAMILY. JUST BECAUSE YOU HAVE THE SAME BLOODLINE DON'T MAKE YOU FAMILY SO KEEP ON BUILDING A FANBASE AND COMMUNITY.

11 - ALWAYS KEEP IN MIND, AS AN UP AND COMING ARTIST THERE ARE GOING TO BE WAY MORE RUTHLESS PEOPLE IN THE MUSIC INDUSTRY THAN IN THE STREETS BECAUSE IN THE MUSIC INDUSTRY, THEY USE PAPERWORK AND IN THE STREETS THEY USE VIOLENCE SO KEEP MORE THAN ONE LAWER ON YOUR TEAM. THAT WAY, YOU CAN BE PROTECTED FROM BOTH SIDES, THE STREETS AND THE MUSIC INDUSTRY.

12 - IF YOU DON'T BELIEVE THAT YOU ARE THE BEST UP AND COMING ARTIST IN THE WORLD THEN NO ONE ELSE IN THE WORLD WILL BELIEVE IT EITHER SO START TAKING ACTION WITH YOUR GOALS AND MUSIC SO THAT YOUR FANS CAN SEE THAT THE BEST YOU HAVE IS YET TO COME AND THAT IT'S GOING TO CHANGE THE WAY THEY SEE YOU BY BELIEVING IN THE POWER OF SELF.

13 - START CUTTING OUT ALL OF THE DISTRACTIONS UNTIL YOU PUT OR GET YOURSELF IN A POSITION OF POWER TO WIN AS A MAJOR ARTIST OR, YOU CAN REMAIN AN INDEPENDENT ARTIST THAT OWNS 100% OF THEIR CATALOG ALONG WITH YOUR MASTERS. NOW YOU WILL HAVE TOTAL CONTROL OF YOUR MUSIC CAREER AND THAT MEANS RECORD LABELS WILL HAVE NO OWNERSHIP AT ALL.

14 - IF YOU ARE NOT HONEST WITH YOURSELF YOU WILL REMAIN DISHONEST WITH THE FANS YOU WILL COME CROSS IN LIFE AND IN THE MUSIC BUSINESS AND THAT'S NOT GOOD BUSINESS. THAT'S PERSONAL SO DO THE RIGHT THING WITH YOUR HONESTY AND YOUR BRAND WILL BECOME SO BIG YOU WILL LOOK LIKE A MAJOR ARTIST WHO IS READY TO BE SIGNED.

15 - THERE ARE NO RECORD LABELS OUT THERE THAT OWE YOU ANYTHING SO STOP LOOKING FOR HANDOUTS AND PUT IN THAT WORK SO YOU CAN REMAIN DEBT FREE SO WHEN THE RECORD LABELS START KNOCKING ON YOUR DOOR FOR THAT PARTNERSHIP, YOU STILL HAVE CONTROL WITHOUT NO HANDOUTS.

16 - START LEARNING HOW TO BRAND AND MARKET YOURSELF TO POINT OTHER BRANDS WILL KNOCK AT YOUR DOOR TO GIVE YOU A BIG BRAND DEAL THAT YOU CAN USE TO REFUEL AND ALSO CHANGE YOUR LIFE FOREVER. THAT CAN BE A DREAM COME TRUE FOR YOUR MUSIC CAREER AS AN UP AND COMING ARTIST SO BE SMART. THINK SMART AND GOD WILL HAVE YOUR BACK.

17 - DON'T STOP GRINDING BECAUSE YOU NEVER KNOW WHERE YOUR MUSIC IS GOING TO TAKE YOU LIKE ON TOUR ALL AROUND THE WORLD MEETING NEW PEOPLE OR OTHER ARTISTS THAT CAN CHANGE YOUR LIFE FOR THE BEST. SO KEEP GOING KEEP TRAVELING, KEEP GRINDING UNTIL YOU CAN'T BE STOPPED BECAUSE BEING AN UP AND COMING ARTIST TAKES WORK SO BE ABOUT YOUR ACTION AND EVERYTHING WILL FALL INTO PLACE.

18 - DON'T TAKE IT PERSONAL WHEN YOUR FAMILY AND FRIENDS DON'T SUPPORT YOU OR YOUR MUSIC BECAUSE STRANGERS WILL SUPPORT YOU FIRST AND THEY ARE AROUND THE CORNER IF YOU STAY FOCUSED TO THE POINT YOU HAVE BUILT A FANBASE FULL OF STRANGERS THAT WILL TURN YOU INTO A MILLIONAIRE OVERNIGHT. JUST DON'T STOP AND YOU WILL POP.

19 - DON'T LISTEN TO OTHERS ARTISTS WHO ARE NOT BEING TRUE IN THEIR MUSIC OR TO THEMSELVES. THEY ARE NOT BEING ORGANIC. THEY ARE NOT STANDING OUT FROM OTHER ARTISTS AND THAT CAN HURT YOUR MUSIC CAREER AS A NEW UP AND COMING ARTIST SO DON'T TRY TO BLEND IN WITH THE CROWD. ALWAYS REMAIN ORGANIC AT ALL TIMES AND YOUR FANS WILL PICK YOU AND STREAM YOUR MUSIC ALL THE TIME.

20 - START BELIEVE IN YOURSELF EVEN IF THE ONES CLOSEST TO YOU DON'T BECAUSE AT THE END OF THE DAY, GOD GAVE YOU THE VISION TO BECOME A GREAT ARTIST THAT THE WORLD NEEDS TO SEE AND HEAR NOW BECAUSE BELIEVING IN SELF IS EMPOWERING AND THAT WILL MAKE YOU BECOME THAT BOSS YOU DREAM OF BECOMING. SO HAVE MORE THAN ONE VISION AND THAT IS CALLED OPENING YOUR THIRD EYE WITH A VISION YOU BELIEVE IN.

21 - START MAKING SURE THE PEOPLE ON YOUR TEAM PLAY THEIR POSITION BECAUSE EVERYBODY NOWADAYS WANTS TO BE THE BOSS WITHOUT PUTTING IN THE WORK LIKE A BOSS AND THAT CAN BE A BIG PROBLEM WHEN YOU ARE STARTING OR BUILDING A TEAM. AS AN UP AND COMING ARTIST, THERE ARE GOING TO BE PEOPLE WHO WILL COME AND GO BUT LET THEM KNOW THAT YOU ARE HERE TO STAY AS A BOSS.

22 - DON'T BE THE TYPE OF ARTIST WHO DOESN'T HIRE SECURITY JUST TO LOOK LIKE A GANGSTER BECAUSE YOUR SAFTY COMES FIRST AND NOT YOUR COOL SO DON'T BE THAT ARTIST WHO DIES OVER TRYING TO LOOK COOL. START BEING SMART WITH YOUR LIFE AND THAT WILL MAKE YOU LOOK COOL TO YOUR FANS FOREVER.

23 - IF YOU HAVE TO REINVENT YOUR OWN WHEEL JUST TO GET RICH OR WEALTHY, START ROLLING THAT WHEEL NOW IN DIFFERENT LANES TO YOUR OWN SUCCESS BECAUSE THE RECORD LABELS DON'T WAIT FOR ANYBODY UNLESS THEY KNOW THAT YOU CAN PRODUCE MILLIONS OF DOLLARS FOR THEM. SO START BUILDING THE BIGGEST BUZZ FOR YOURSELF BY WORD OF MOUTH, WORD ON THE STREETS, SOCIAL MEDIA, BLOGGERS AND OTHER MARKETING AND PROMOTION OUTLETS.

24 - DON'T BE AFRAID TO FAIL. YOUR SUCCESS IS GOING TO COME FROM NOT GIVING UP AND STAYING CONSISTENT AS AN UP AND COMING ARTIST GIVING YOU THE POWER TO COME UP AND WALK IN THE MUSIC INDUSTRY WITH MORE LEVERAGE THAN ANY OTHER ARTIST THAT COMES AFTER YOU SO RECORD AS MUCH MUSIC AS YOU CAN SO THAT YOU CAN KEEP YOUR FOOT ON THESE RECORD LABELS' NECKS.

25 - START BUILDING A FANBASE LOCALLY AND GLOBALLY BY STANDING OUT FROM OTHER ARTISTS AROUND YOU BY USING CONTENT BECAUSE RIGHT NOW, CONTENT IS KING AND FANS WANT TO SEE HOW YOU ARE LIVING AND WHAT YOU DO ON A DAILY BASIS. SO START FILMING YOUR OWN DAY IN THE LIFE VLOG VIDEOS TO BUILD A BIGGER FANBASE FOR YOUR MUSIC CAREER.

26 - THE RECORDS LABELS WILL ONLY TREAT YOU HOW YOU FEEL ABOUT YOURSELF SO KEEP ON ADDING MORE VALUE TO YOURSELF. THAT WAY YOU REMAIN MORE VALUABLE THAN OTHER UP AND COMING ARTISTS THAT THE RECORDS LABELS ARE LOOKING TO SIGN BECAUSE THE RECORDS LABELS ARE LOOKING AT THE NUMBERS AND HOW MUCH INFLUENCE YOU HAVE IN THE WORLD SO THEY CAN MAKE MILLIONS OF DOLLARS JUST OFF OF YOUR INFLUENCE ALONE.

27 - DON'T WORRY ABOUT BEING A PERFECT ARTIST. JUST FOCUS MORE ON BEING A REAL ARTIST TO YOURSELF AND NOT TO THE MUSIC INDUSTRY BECAUSE THEY DON'T HAVE YOUR BACK LIKE YOU WOULD HAVE YOUR OWN BACK. THAT'S WHEN THE INDEPENDENT MINDSET COMES INTO PLAY AS YOU MAKE YOUR OWN PLAYLIST TO GET YOUR MUSIC OUT THERE TO THE WORLD.

28 - START LEARNING TO TAKE RISKS AS AN UP COMING ARTIST OR YOU WILL ALWAYS WORK FOR THE RECORD LABELS AND BE A SLAVE FOREVER. LEARN HOW TO BUILD A BOSS MINDSET TO TAKE YOU OUT OF THAT SLAVE MINDSET. SO START YOUR OWN RECORD LABEL AND THEN GO FIFTY/FIFTY WITH OTHER LABELS OR BUILD YOUR OWN RECORD LABEL WITH YOUR OWN TEAM AND YOU WILL NEVER BE A SLAVE TO OTHER RECORD LABELS AGAIN.

29 - KEEP ON GETTING KNOWLEDGE ABOUT THE MUSIC INDUSTRY BECAUSE IT WILL GIVE YOU MORE POWER AS AN UP AND COMING ARTIST. ALSO, HAVE GOOD CHARACTER SO THAT WHEN YOUR RESPECT COMES INTO PLAY AS YOU BUILD YOUR OWN MINDSET TO A NEW LEVEL THAT CAN'T BE STOPPED OR PLAYED WITH AT ALL. SO INVEST YOUR TIME IN READING BOOKS ABOUT THE MUSIC INDUSTRY AND DO MORE RESEARCH ON THE INTERNET SO THAT YOU CAN'T LOSE, ONLY GAIN, AND THAT'S REAL SHIT.

30 - BUILDING YOUR OWN NAME OR A BUZZ DOESN'T HAVE TO END RIGHT THERE. WHEN YOU DROP NEW MUSIC, LIKE AN EP, ALBUM OR SINGLE, IT JUST MEANS YOU ARE JUST GETTING STARTED AND YOUR NAME IS STARTING TO GROW IN THE STREETS, INTERNET, SOCIAL MEDIA, AND IN THE MUSIC INDUSTRY. NOW, BEING THAT UP AND COMING ARTIST WHO IS NEW, THE ATTENTION WILL BE ON YOU BECAUSE YOU STAND OUT WITH DIFFERENT TYPES OF MUSIC THAT YOUR FANS LOVE.

31 - ONCE YOU KNOW HOW SOMEONE IS IN THE MUSIC INDUSTRY DON'T PUT THEM IN THE POSITION TO LET YOU DOWN BECAUSE AT THE END OF THE DAY YOU ARE THE ONE THAT IS BUILDING YOUR OWN MUSIC CAREER SO CONTINUE TO SEARCH FOR THE RIGHT PEOPLE OR THE RIGHT PERSON TO GET THE BALL ROLLING SO THAT YOU CAN PUT HIM OR HER IN THE POSITION OF POWER TO HELP YOU TO TAKE OVER THE WORLD WITH YOUR OWN RECORD LABEL.

32 - THE HARDEST THING WHEN IT COMES TO BEING A NEW ARTIST IS THAT PEOPLE AROUND YOU DON'T WANT TO GROW OR WILL NOT GROW WITH YOU AS YOU BECOME SUCCESSFUL BECAUSE THEY DON'T BELIEVE IN THEMSELVES. YOU DO SO KEEP ON GROWING, SHINING, BUILDING AND LIVING YOUR DREAMS TO THE FULLEST. KEEP IT TO YOURSELF AS YOU REMAIN MORE POWERFUL IN TIME.

33 - START LEARNING YOUR OWN SECRETS TO YOUR OWN SUCCESS. THAT WAY, WHEN PEOPLE ASK YOU ABOUT YOUR JOURNEY AS AN UP AND COMING ARTIST, YOU CAN BREAK IT DOWN SECRET BY SECRET WHEN THEY DO FACE-TO-FACE INTERVIEWS WITH YOU AS AN UP AND COMING ARTIST. MAKE SURE YOU GIVE YOUR FANS THE REAL YOU WITH NO BULLSHIT.

34 - DON'T LET ANYONE TRICK YOU OUTTA YOUR POSITION BECAUSE LOSING EVERYTHING THAT YOU BUILT OVER TIME AS A NEW ARTIST WILL NOT BE WORTH IT BECAUSE TIME IS NOT GOING BE YOUR BEST FRIEND AT ALL. AND IF ANYONE IS TRYING TO TRICK YOU OUT OF YOUR POSITION, THAT MEANS THEY WANT TO BE YOU SO BAD AND THAT COULD BE A GOOD THING OR A BAD THING. IT'S ALL IN HOW YOU SEE IT.

35 - THE NUMBER ONE, BIGGEST KEY TO BEING SUCCESSFUL AS AN UP AND COMING ARTIST IN 2023 AND 2024, BESIDES MAKING GOOD MUSIC IS BRANDING YOURSELF BECAUSE IT'S YOUR OWN PERSONAL BRAND THAT THE WORLD NEEDS TO SEE GROW WITH THE BAD, THE GOOD, OR UGLY THAT CAN MAKE YOU RICH OR WEALTHY AS YOUR TIME GOES ON SO YOU GOTTA MAKE IT HAPPEN NOW.

36 - START SELLING YOUR OWN MERCH ONLINE BECAUSE IT CAN HELP YOU MAKE MORE ADDITIONAL REVENUE. AS A NEW ARTIST AND YOU CAN REACH MORE FANS OR BUILD A FANBASE LOCALLY AND AROUND THE WORLD BECAUSE BUILDING YOUR BRAND AS AN UP AND COMING ARTIST WILL BRING YOU EVEN MORE OPPORTUNITIES WITH OTHER COMPANIES THAT ARE ON THE COME-UP JUST LIKE YOU.

37 - IF YOU WANT FAMILY AND FRIENDS TO BELIEVE IN YOUR DREAMS OR VISION AND ALL OF YOUR IDEAS YOU HAVE TO STARTING SHOWING THEM INSTEAD OF TELLING THEM ABOUT IT EVERY DAY BECAUSE THE EYES WILL LISTEN MORE THAN EARS SO KEEP ON SHOWING YOUR VISION TO THE POINT YOU HAVE YOUR OWN TEAM.

38 - DON'T RUN AROUND BLAMING SOMEONE IN THE MUSIC BUSINESS FOR YOUR OWN IGNORANCE BECAUSE THERE ARE BOOKS, MENTORS AND EVEN YOUTUBE VIDEOS THAT CAN AND WILL EDUCATE YOU TO A WHOLE NEW LEVEL WITH GAME AS A NEW ARTIST SO REMAIN GRINDING TO THE TOP. THAT WAY YOU CAN START EDUCATING OTHER ARTISTS THAT WANT TO LEVEL UP WITH THEIR MUSC CAREER.

39 - NO MATTER WHAT IS GOING ON IN YOUR LIFE, YOU HAVE TO CREATE YOUR OWN LANE IN THE MUSIC INDUSTRY. THAT WAY YOU STAND OUT IN A BRANDING WAY TO THE POINT THERE IS NO STOPPING YOU OR THE PEOPLE AROUND YOU SO KEEP CREATING MORE LANES AS YOU DRIVE YOUR WAY TO SUCCESS.

40 - STOP FOCUSING ON THE WRONG THINGS WHEN YOU ARE TRYING TO BUILD A FANBASE THAT WILL NEVER LEAVE YOUR SIDE IN GOOD TIMES OR IN BAD TIMES. SO GET TO WORK NOW SO WHEN YOU GO ON TOUR, YOUR SHOWS WILL BE FULL WITH 3,000 TO 5,000 FANS THAT WILL BUY ANYTHING THAT YOU ARE SELLING, LIKE T-SHIRTS, HATS, COFFEE CUPS AND MORE. SO REMAIN FOCUSED AND YOU WILL WIN.

41 - START INVESTING JUST ABOUT EVERY DOLLAR THAT YOU EVER MADE INTO YOUR MUSIC CAREER. THAT WAY, YOUR R.O.I. WILL BE BIGGER THAN THE INVESTMENT YOU PUT IN FROM THE BEGINNING AND YOUS SHOULD BECOME RICHER THAN OTHER ARTITS THAT ARE IN THE GAME OR ARTISTS THAT ARE COMING INTO THE GAME AS TIME GOES ON WITH MORE INVESTMENT.

42 - ALWAY REMEMBER TO REMAIN A STUDENT OF TO THE MUSIC BUSINESS. THAT WAY YOU CAN KEEP LEARNING NEW THINGS THAT WILL TAKE YOU TO THE NEXT LEVEL AND THAT IS WHA'TS UP BECAUSE THERE ARE OTHER ARTISTS WHO DON'T LIKE TO LISTEN AND THAT'S WHY THEIR MUSIC CAREER NEVER TOOK OFF. THAT WILL NOT BE THE CASE WITH YOU BECAUSE YOU ARE GOING TO BE DIFFERENT FROM THE REST OF THEM.

43 - START TO LEARN THIS WORD "EMBRACE" BECAUSE YOU CAN GAIN SO MUCH WISDOM FROM THOSE WHO HAVE BEEN THERE BEFORE YOU IN THE MUSIC BUSINESS. SO LEARN AS MUCH AS YOU CAN. THAT WAY YOUR MUSIC CAREER CAN GROW BIGGER THAN A JAY-Z, 50 CENT, DAME DASH AND THE LIST GOES ON. SO EMBRACE THE GAME AND PUT YOUR OWN MONEY UP.

44 - START LEARNING TO BE MORE CAREFUL WITH YOUR WORDS BECAUSE ONCE THEY'VE BECOME A SONG, THEY WILL NOT BE FORGOTTEN AFTER YOU RELEASE IT. IT WILL START TO IMPACT OTHER PEOPLE'S MINDS AND THAT IS A POWERFUL THING IN A POSITIVE WAY OR IN NEGATIVE WAY SO ONLY YOU CAN MAKE THAT CHOICE WHEN IT COMES TO WORDS AND THEN YOU WILL FIND YOUR TRUE INNER SELF.

45 - LEARN TO USE SOCIAL MEDIA TO BUILD YOUR OWN COMMUNITY AS A NEW UP AND COMING ARTIST BECAUSE WHEN YOU SERVE YOUR COMMUNITY, THEY WILL SERVE YOU BY FUNDING YOUR CAMPAIGNS AND GROWING YOUR FANBASE FROM THEIR WORD OF MOUTH. THAT IS THE BIGGEST MARKETING TOOL EVER BECAUSE WORDS ARE POWERFUL WHEN YOU ARE USING SOCIAL MEDIA AS YOUR BIGGEST TOOL TO PUSH THEM.

46 - DON'T BURN NO BRIDGES IN THE MUSIC INDUSTRY BECAUSE BEING BLACKBALLED DOESN'T FEEL OR LOOK GOOD WHEN YOU ARE BUILDING YOUR OWN BRAND AS AN UP AND COMING ARTIST SO CONTINUE TO BUILD GOOD RELATIONSHIPS AND BE REAL TO YOURSELF AND THINGS SHOULD FALL IN PLACE AS YOU MEET PEOPLE IN THE MUSIC INDUSTRY THAT CAN CHANGE THE WAY YOU LIVE FOREVER.

47 - ALWAYS REMEMBER YOUR SELF IMAGE IS VERY IMPORTANT AS AN UP AND COMING ARTIST BECAUSE IT IS GOING TO BE YOUR STARTING POINT TO BRAND YOURSELF SO PEOPLE CAN SEE YOU IN A DIFFERENT LIGHT AND THAT'S WHEN A&R'S AND RECORDS LABELS WILL START REACHING OUT TO YOU ON SOME REAL BUSINESS SHIT. SO, FOCUS ON YOUR IMAGE BECAUSE PEOPLE WILL BUY INTO YOUR IMAGE FIRST BEFORE THEY BUY YOUR MUSIC.

48 - START LEARNING THE INS AND OUTS WHEN IT COMES TO MARKETING,BRANDING,PROMOTI ON AND ADVERTING BECAUSE IT CAN TAKE YOUR MUSIC CAREER TO THE NEXT LEVEL AS AN UP AND COMING ARTIST. AND, IT CAN MAKE YOU LOOK BIGGER THAN LIFE AS AN UP AND COMING ARTIST SO STAY DOWN SO YOU COME UP IN THE MUSIC GAME.

49 - DON'T JOIN NO TYPE OF GANG AFTER YOU BECOME SUCCESSFUL WITH YOUR MUSIC CAREER BECAUSE YOU DON'T WANT TO GO TO JAIL OR DIE TRYING TO BE A PART OF SOMETHING THAT DON'T LOVE YOU, OR HAS NO TYPE OF LOVE FOR YOUR DREAMS, GOALS, VISION THAT YOU BUILT OVER THE YEARS SO REMAIN GANG FREE AT ALL TIMES.

50 - START MAKING A DIFFERENCE IN YOUR COMMUNITY BECAUSE IF YOU DO, YOU CAN CHANGE THE WAY PEOPLE THINK AND MORE. WHEN IT COMES TO THIS MUSIC INDUSTRY AND THIS THING CALLED LIFE, YOU CAN'T SEPARATE YOURSELF FROM IT BECAUSE THEY GO HAND IN HAND TOGETHER LIKE A RELATIONSHIP SO KEEP ON BUILDING YOUR OWN COMMUNITY AND YOU WILL BE A SUCCESSFUL UP AND COMING ARTIST IN NO TIME.

51 - THERE ARE GOING TO BE THREE ESSENTIAL THINGS THAT ARTISTS SHOULD NOT BE DOING AND THOSE ARE WASTING TIME, MONEY OR EXPERIENCES BECAUSE ALL THREE OF THOSE THINGS CAN CHANGE YOUR LIFE IF YOU LEARN HOW TO USE AND VALUE THEM THE RIGHT WAY AS YOU BUILD AND GROW YOUR MUSIC CAREER TO THE END AS TIME GOES ON WITH MORE ESSENTIAL THINGS.

52 - THERE ARE A LOT OF ARTISTs NOWADAYS WHO RUN FROM THEIR GODGIVEN TALENT. ALL THEY NEED TO DO IS JUST HUSTLE AND FLOW WITH IT AND GO HARD. TRUST YOURSELF BECAUSE GOD GOT YOUR BACK TO MAKE SURE YOU STAY ON YOUR GRIND TO LET YOU KNOW THAT THE WORLD IS YOURS. SO DON'T GIVE UP. KEEP GOING BECAUSE SUCCESS FOR YOU IS AROUND THE CORNER.

53 - START BEING THAT ARTIST WHO BRINGS A POWERFUL VOICE TO THE MUSIC INDUSTRY THAT MAY CHANGE THE GAME FOREVER. SO, BE THAT SOURCE, THAT HARD TO FIND VOICE TO CREATE LOYALTY WITH A REAL AUDIENCE THAT LOVES YOUR ART. THAT MAY CHANGE OTHER ARTIST'S MINDSET FOREVER AS YOU LEVEL UP WITH A REAL VISION THAT YOU CANNOT BUY ANYWHERE.

54 - THERE ARE NO RESULTS
WITHOUT PERSISTENCE SO GOING
HARD CAN AND WILL PAY OFF. JUST
DON'T STOP BECAUSE IT'S TIME TO
BE THAT STAR THAT GOD WANTED
YOU TO BE AND PUTTING IN THAT
WORK MAKES DREAMS AND GOALS
COME TRUE IF YOU BELIEVE IN
YOURSELF FROM THE BEGINNING
OF TIME TO THE END OF TIME.

55 - ALWAYS REMEMBER THAT YOUR BIGGEST BREAK IS GOING TO COME WHEN YOU GRIND SMARTER THAN OTHER ARTIST'S AND HARDER THAN THEM. THEY WON'T STAND OUT LIKE YOU. THAT MEANS IT'S TIME FOR SOME ACTION ON YOUR BEHALF THAT WILL HAVE THE RECORD LABELS THAT DIDN'T BELIEVE IN YOU WHEN YOU HAD THAT FACE-TO-FACE OFFICE MEETING WITH THEM CALLING YOUR PHONE.

56 - START WRITING DOWN ALL YOUR GOALS YOU WANT TO ACCOMPLISH FOR YOUR MUSIC CAREER BECAUSE YOUR GOALS OR PLANS THAT YOU SET UP FOR YOURSELF ARE VALUABLE. IT'S TIME FOR YOU TO STOP MAKING EXCUSES AND PRODUCING RESULTS THAT CAN CHANGE YOUR LIFE AND THE LIVES OF THE PEOPLE AROUND YOU.

57 - START YOUR OWN 90-DAY BLUEPRINT THAT WILL TEACH YOU HOW TO BUILD A STRONG BRAND AND GROW YOUR FANBASE AT THE SAME TIME BY CREATING CONTENT THAT RESONATES WITH YOUR AUDIENCE. THIS IS A BLUE PRINT YOU NEED TO STAY CONSISTENT WITH. AT TIMES, POSTING CONTENT EVERY DAY WILL HELP YOU BUILD YOUR BRAND AS AN UP AND COMING ARTIST IN THE INTERNET WORLD.

58 - START USING ANYONE WHO HAS EVER DOUBTED YOU AS AN UP AND COMING ARTIST AS FUEL OR GAS TO MAKE YOU SUCCESSFUL AS TIME GOES ON BECAUSE DREAMS DO COME TRUE AND WORDS ARE POWERFUL. JUST REMEMBER, THE WORDS THAT ARE COMING OUTTA YOUR MOUTH MEAN YOU HAVE THE POWER TO PRODUCE THEM SO KEEP PRODUCING NEW WORDS THAT GIVE YOU POWER.

59 - START WATCHING A LOT OF YOUTUBE VIDEOS TO LEARN THE BREAKDOWN OF THE MUSIC INDUSTRY SO THAT YOU CAN BE ON TOP OF YOUR GAME WITHOUT BEING GAMED OR CLUELESS IN A CORRUPTED INDUSTRY THAT DOESN'T HAVE YOUR BACK. THAT'S WHEN YOU COME IN TO PLAY WITH THAT BOSS MINDSET AND ARTIST THAT THE WORD 'NO' IS NOT ONE OF YOUR GOALS.

60 - DON'T SELL YOUR SOUL TO THE DEVIL JUST FOR A FEW MILLION DOLLARS THAT YOU CAN MAKE ON YOUR OWN BECAUSE YOU ARE THE BRAND SO START ADDING MORE VALUE TO YOURSELF SO THAT YOU CAN BECOME THAT MILLIONAIRE THAT YOU DREAMED ABOUT BECOMING WITH YOUR OWN ADVANCE MONEY OUT OF YOUR OWN POCKET.

61 - IT'S YOUR DUTY AS A NEW ARTIST TO REFLECT YOUR OWN MINDSET TO MIND YOUR OWN BUSINESS. IT IS TIME FOR YOU TO TAKE ACTION THAT IS GOING TO IMPACT THE WORLD WHILE YOU ARE STILL LIVING OR WHEN YOU DIE. YOUR IMPACT MUST BE SO POWERFUL THAT WHEN YOU DIE YOUR FANS STILL THINK YOU ARE STILL LIVING. NOW THAT'S A POWERFUL IMPACT THAT CANNOT BE STOPPED.

62 - SOMETIMES THE THING THAT WILL HOLD YOU BACK IN LIFE IS A WEAK MINDSET SO BUILD A STRONGER MINDSET SO THAT YOU CAN GO AGAINST THE WORLD AND OTHER PEOPLE WHO DON'T SEE YOUR VISION AS YOU BECOME THE GREATEST ARTIST IN THE WORLD WITH A RECORD LABEL OR WITHOUT A RECORD LABEL. ONLY TIME WILL TELL HOW STRONG YOUR MINDSET HAS BECOME WITH THE CHANGES YOU HAVE MADE.

63 - ALWAYS REMEMBER WHO IGNORED YOU WHEN YOU FIRST WANTED TO MAKE MUSIC AND WHOEVER HELPED YOU BEFORE YOU EVEN HAD TO ASK THEM FOR ANY TYPE OF HELP WHEN IT CAME TO YOUR MUSIC. LET THEM KEEP THAT SAME ENERGY WHILE YOU CHANGE YOUR ENERGY TO NEW ENERGY TO HELP OTHER ARTISTS BUILD THEIR OWN ENERGY.

64 - NEVER FORGET OTHER ARTISTS THAT YOU HAVE SEEN YOU AT THEIR LOWEST POINT. THOSE ARE THE TYPES OF ARTISTS WHO YOU OFFER NO TYPE OF JUDGEMENT. INSTEAD, EXTENDED TO THEM SOME REAL GOOD INFORMATION, GEMS, GAME, THAT WOULD PUT THEM ON A LEVEL LIKE YOU AS TIME GOES ON. NOBODY IN THE RECORD LABLES WILL NOT SEE IT COMING FROM A MILE AWAY.

65 - YOU MUST UNDERSTAND, AS AN UNSIGNED ARTIST, BRANDING YOURSELF IS THE FIRST THING THAT YOU SHOULD DO BECAUSE YOU HAVE TO SET YOURSELF APART FROM EVERY OTHER ARTIST THAT IS COMING UP IN THE MUSIC INDUSTRY BEFORE YOU, WITH YOU AND AFTER YOU. SO AT THE END OF THE DAY, BRANDING SHOULD BE FIRST ON YOUR LIST.

66 - WHEN YOU ARE A NEW ARTIST COMING INTO THE MUSIC INDUSTRY, YOU CANNOT TAKE ANY BREAKS BECAUSE THERE ARE GOING TO BE OTHERS ARTISTS OUT THERE WHO WILL PUSH YOU OUT THE WAY FROM YOUR OWN ALGORITHMS THAT YOU BUILT WITH OWN DATA SO STAY ON GRIND MODE AND CONTINUE TO RUN YOUR OWN SHOW.

67 - SOMETIMES, AS A NEW ARTIST THAT BEEN GRINDING FOR A WHILE, YOU NEED TO START DISAPPEARING FROM THE MUSIC INDUSTRY SO THAT YOUR HATERS CAN THINK THAT YOU FELL OFF. THEN COME BACK TO TAKE OVER THE INDUSTRY WITH SO MANY NEW PROJECTS LIKE MUSIC VIDEOS, INTERVIEWS, CLOTHING LINES, TV SHOWS, REALITY SHOWS, BOOK AND MORE.

68 - START LEARNING TO STAY AWAY FROM NEGATIVE PEOPLE LIKE FAKE FRIENDS OR FAMILY MEMBERS BECAUSE NEGATIVE ENERGY IS REAL AS YOU START TO BUILD YOUR MUSIC CAREER. STAY FOCUSED SO THAT YOU CAN GO TO THE NEXT LEVEL WITH YOUR MUSIC CAREER AND THAT'S A POSITIVE LEVEL. SOME PEOPLE ARE GOING TO NEED SOME TYPE OF PASSWORD OR KEYWORDS TO ENTER YOUR CIRCLE.

69 - START USING YOUR SHOW MONEY TO PAY BACK THE RECORD LABEL'S ADVANCE MONEY. THAT WAY YOU CAN BE DEBT FREE AS TIME GOES ON WITH MUSIC CAREER SO YOU CAN DROP NEW MUSIC ANYTIME YOU WANT AND THAT'S WHEN YOU START YOUR OWN RECORD LABEL AS YOU BECOME MORE DEBT FREE.

70 - START SIGNING UP FOR YOUR OWN LIFE INSURANCE POLICY ASAN UP AND COMING ARTIST JUST CASE YOU DIE. THAT WAY, ALL OF YOUR LIFE INSURANCE MONEY CAN GO TO YOUR FAMILY OR KIDS AND NOT THE RECORD LABELS BECAUSE THEY ARE RICH ENOUGH AND NOW IT'S YOUR TURN NOW.

71 - BUILDING YOUR OWN FAN BASE DOESN'T HAVE TO START WITH SOCIAL MEDIA. IT CAN START WITH YOUR OWN SELF-CONFIDENCE WHEN YOU BELIEVE IN YOURSELF AS AN ARTIST AND THAT'S WHEN OPPORTUNITIES WILL START TO KNOCK ON DOOR AS YOU BUILD YOUR BRAND AND THAT BRAND IS YOU.

72 - DON'T STOP GRINDING WHEN YOU COME TO YOUR FIRST SIGN OF SUCCESS BECAUSE YOU WILL BECOME STAGNANT AND LAZY. YOU MUST WORK EVEN HARDER SO THAT YOUR MUSIC CAREER HAS NO TYPE OF BREAKS IN BETWEEN OR ANY TYPE OF ROOM FOR FAILURE. SO GRIND SMART BY DOING THINGS THAT MAKE YOU STAND OUT FROM OTHER ARTISTS THAT ARE ON THE COME-UP AS WELL AND YOU WILL BE THE MOST TALKED ABOUT ON THE INTERNET AND IN THE STREETS.

73 - ALWAYS REMEMBER YOUR OWN SUCCESS WILL START IN YOUR OWN MIND SO BE CONSISTENT WITH YOUR GRIND. THAT WAY, YOU CAN BE READY TO SHINE AS YOU CONTINUE TO PUT THAT WORK IN AS A NEW ARTIST ON THE COME-UP IN THE MUSIC INDUSTRY BECAUSE PUTTING IN THAT WORK IS GOING TO BE EMPOWERING.

74 - DON'T EVER LET ANY RECORD LABEL OR A&R TELL YOU THAT YOU ARE NOT THE GREATEST. BE THAT ARTIST TO CLAIM THAT YOU ARE THE GREATEST AND WATCH THE OUTCOME WHEN YOU TELL YOURSELF THAT EVERY DAY WHEN YOU GO TO BED AND WHEN YOU WAKE UP IN THE MORNING.

75 - IF YOU ARE AN UP AND COMING ARTIST AND YOU ARE TAKING YOUR MUSIC CAREER MORE SERIOUSLY THAN EVER, THAT MEANS YOU ARE ON THE RIGHT TRACK SO STAY HUNGRY FOR KNOWLEDGE AND KEEP GOD FIRST AND THE OUTCOME WILL BECOME YOUR POWER THAT CAN AND WILL CHANGE THE MINDS OF OTHER THAT YOU MEET ON THE WAY UP.

76 - START DEVELOPING YOUR OWN SUCCESSFUL HABITS WITH BIG GOALS AND DREAMS AS AN UP AND COMING ARTIST. THAT WAY YOU KNOW YOUR OWN LANE IN THE DARK AND IN THE LIGHT OF THE MUSIC BUSINESS SO DO IT NOW WHILE YOU ARE BUILDING YOUR WEALTH SO THAT YOU CAN'T BE STOPPED.

77 - START STANDING ON YOUR OWN TWO FEET AND DON'T DEPEND ON ANYONE OR ANYTHING FOR YOUR OWN SUCCESS BECAUSE MEN WILL LET YOU DOWN WHILE THE WOMEN WANT YOU TO WIN BECAUSE YOUR WIN IS HER WIN. THAT'S WHEN YOU AND HER TAKE OVER THE WORLD WITH FOUR FEET.

78 - DON'T SELL YOURSELF SO CHEAP LIKE SOME OF THESE ARTISTS DO BECAUSE YOU ARE WORTH EXACTLY WHAT YOU SAY YOU ARE WORTH. AS YOU SEE YOUR FULL POTENTIAL WITH HEALTH, WEALTH, HAPPINESS, LOVE, SUCCESS, MONEY AND MORE TO COME AS YOU BUILD MORE POTENTIAL WAYS.

79 - START LEARNING TO GET AWAY FROM THE CROWD OR A PERSON THAT'S AT THE BOTTOM BUT AT THE SAME TIME, LEARN FROM THAT PERSON WHO IS AT THE BOTTOM AS WELL. THAT WAY, YOU CAN USE THEIR FAILURES AS FUEL TO BE SUCCESSFUL AS YOU BUILD YOUR MUSIC CAREER AS AN UP AND COMING ARTIST WORLDWIDE.

80 - THERE ARE GOING BE PEOPLE OR OTHER ARTISTS WHO HATE ON YOU AS YOU BUILD YOUR MUSIC CAREER. THEY ONLY HATE ON YOU BECAUSE THERE ARE SOME THINGS THAT THEY ARE MISSING IN THEM THAT THEY SEE IN YOU SO KEEP ON GRINDING AND SHINING AND ONLY TIME WILL TELL AS YOU MAKE POWER MOVES.

81 - START LEARNING OR FIND WAYS TO CONNECT WITH YOUR FANBASE SO THAT YOU CAN TURN THEM INTO YOUR OWN COMMUNITY OF CONSUMERS AS YOU REP YOUR BRAND AS A MUSIC ARTIST THAT WILL NOT TAKE NO FOR ANSWER BECAUSE ONE YES FROM THE RIGHT PERSON CAN CHANGE YOUR LIFE.

82 - DON'T EXPECT RECORDS LABELS, A&R'S, MUSIC PRODUCERS, RADIO, DEEJAY'S, FAMILY, OR FRIENDS TO SEE YOUR VISION AS CLEAR AS YOU DO BECAUSE PEOPLE LISTEN WITH THEIR EYES AND NOT WITH THEY EARS SO KEEP ON MAKING NOISE UNTIL THEY PAY ATTENTION TO YOUR VISION.

83 – LISTEN TO OTHER GENRES OF MUSIC OUTSIDE OF THE GENRE YOU CREATE. THAT WILL HELP YOU TO CREATE A UNIQUE SOUND ALL YOUR OWN.

84 – SUCCESS LEAVES FOOTPRINTS SO STUDY SOME OF THE TECHNIQUES AND TACTICS USED BY UP AND COMING ARTISTS BEFORE YOU. THOSE STRATEGIES CAN HELP YOU REACH YOUR GOALS.

85 - START BEING THE BEST VERSION OF YOURSELF AS AN UP AND COMING ARTIST AND IT STARTS WITH YOUR HEALTH, MINDSET, LOVING YOURSELF, COMMITMENT, ,BELIEF IN YOURSELF AND KEEPING GOD FIRST BECAUSE HE IS GOING TO HAVE YOUR BACK AND BE YOUR BEST FRIEND.

86 - THE PATH TO BEING SUCCESSFUL NEVER STOPS IN THE MUSIC BUSINESS. IN THE MUSIC INDUSTRY, EVERY ARTIST CAN COME IN THE GAME QUICK, FAST, SLOW AND STEADY, UP OR DOWN. IT CAN BE EASY OR COMPLEX SO FIND A WAY TO ACHIEVE YOUR OWN SUCCESS AS AN UNSIGNED ARTIST AND EVERYTHING WITH YOUR MUSIC CAREER WILL FALL INTO PLACE AS TIME GOES ON.

87 - BUILD YOUR OWN PERSONA AS AN UP AND COMING ARTIST WITH A POWERFUL IMPACT BY USING PEOPLE THAT HATE AGAINST YOU AND LET THEM BRING YOU THAT BIG PAY OFF WITH MORE MONEY, SUCCESS AND A NEW LIFESTYLE THAT CAN HELP YOU BUILD YOUR BRAND WITH FREE PROMOTION THAT WOULD HAVE COST MILLIONS OF DOLLARS FROM THE IMPACT OF YOUR HATERS.

88 - THERE ARE ARTISTS OUT THERE NOW WITH A LOT OF GOOD MUSIC BUT DON'T HAVE NO TYPE OF HUSTLE IN THEM BECAUSE IF THEY DID, THEY WOULD GET UP EVERY DAY TO FIGURE THIS MUSIC SHIT OUT OR MAKE A WAY TO MAKE IT HAPPEN. THAT HUSTLE GOT TO BE IN YOU AND NOT ON YOU.

89 - START GOING OUT THERE AND LIVING YOUR DREAMS. STOP ASKING RECORD LABELS PERMISSION OR FROM OTHER PEOPLE WHO ARE NOT LIVING THEIR DREAMS AS AN ARTIST BECAUSE YOU ARE YOUR OWN BOSS. YOU GIVE YOURSELF PERMISSION TO DO WHATEVER YOU WANT TO DO AND THAT IS A BOSS MOVE.

90 - START LEARNING HOW TO BOUNCE BACK WHEN YOU TAKE AN L. AS A NEW ARTIST ON THE COME-UP, IT'S ALL ABOUT MINDSET AND TAKING ACTION WHEN THOSE L 'S COME YOUR WAY SO BELIEVE IT'S ALL ABOUT MINDSET BECAUSE IF YOU HAVE A POWERFUL MINDSET, YOU WILL NEVER TAKE AN L.

91 - START LEARNING HOW TO TRAIN YOUR FANS TO BECOME YOUR BIGGEST CONSUMERS. THAT IS GOING TO BE SO IMPORTANT AS A NEW ARTIST BECAUSE THAT CAN FUND YOUR MUSIC JOURNEY, FUND YOUR MISSION AND FUND YOUR DREAMS UNTIL YOU FUND YOUR OWN.

92 - START LEARNING TO BUILD YOUR OWN GENERATIONAL WEALTH WITH YOUR MUSIC CAREER. THAT WAY YOUR FAMILY OR KIDS CAN LEVERAGE THE WEALTH AFTER YOU LEAVE THE EARTH WITHOUT A FINANCIAL STRUGGLE OR CARE IN THE WORLD AND THAT IS CALLED PASSIVE INCOME FOR LIFE.

93 - START LEARNING SMART THINGS TO DO WITH YOUR SMARTPHONE AS AN UP AND COMING ARTIST, LIKE SHOOTING DAY IN LIFE VIDEOS AND EVERYDAY VLOG VIDEOS AS WELL BECAUSE, BELIEVE OR NOT, PEOPLE WANT TO SEE YOUR LIFESTYLE LIKE WHAT YOU LIKE TO WEAR, EAT AND HEAR YOUR OPINION ABOUT OTHER ARTISTS.

94 - START LEARNING TO STAND ON REAL BUSINESS AS YOU START BUILDING YOUR OWN MUSIC CAREER. THAT WAY YOU CAN PARTNER UP WITH OTHER BOSSES IN THE INDUSTRY OR IN YOUR CITY AND THAT'S WHEN YOU START TO TAKE OVER THE GAME.

95 - START DOING MORE AND STAYING FOCUSED ON THE MISSION THAT CAN CHANGE YOUR LIFE AND OTHER PEOPLE'S LIVES AS WELL. BUILD YOUR MUSIC CAREER FROM THE BOTTOM ALL THE WAY TO THE TOP JUST TO GET A&R'S, MUSIC PRODUCER'S, DEEJAY'S, AND RECORD LABELS' ATTENTION.

96 - START CREATING CONTENT ON YOUR JOURNEY AS YOU BUILD WEALTH BECAUSE CONTENT IS GOING TO BE THE PROOF OF YOUR OWN SUCCESS TO THE WORLD THAT WILL LIVE ON FOREVER. DON'T STOP CREATING CONTENT BECAUSE IT CAN MAKE YOU A VERY RICH ARTIST WITHOUT A RECORD LABEL.

97 - START LEARNING THAT RECORD LABELS DON'T CARE ABOUT TALENT. THEY ONLY CARE ABOUT DATA, SALES, MONEY, PUBLISHING, PLUS MORE BECAUSE YOU MAY ASK YOURSELF OR TELL YOURSELF THAT, "I HAVE TALENT," BUT IT DOESN'T MATTER IF YOU CAN'T SELL RECORDS FOR THEM.

98 - WHEN RECORD LABELS GIVE YOU ADVANCE MONEY, LEARN HOW TO USE IT WISELY. THAT WAY, YOU WON'T BE IN BAD DEBT AND SO MAKE SURE THAT ADVANCE MONEY BECOMES GOOD DEBT. THAT WAY, YOU CAN USE IT OVER AND OVER AS YOUR MUSIC CAREER GOES ON IN TIME.

99 - WHEN YOU UNDERSTAND THAT AS AN UP AND COMING ARTIST, EVERYONE IN THE MUSIC BUSINESS IS THERE TO MAKE MONEY, YOU DON'T TAKE ANYTHING PERSONAL WHILE YOU ARE ON YOUR WAY UP BUILDING YOUR MUSIC CAREER AND YOU WILL BE RICHER THAN RECORD LABELS AND OTHER ARTISTS.

100 - START USING THE POWER OF LEVERAGING YOUR OWN CREDIT BECAUSE YOU CAN REACH AND GROW YOUR MUSIC CAREER MUCH FASTER WHEN YOU PUT TOGETHER YOUR FINANCIAL GOALS AND PLANS. PAYING YOURSELF FIRST IS A GREAT MARKETING, FINANCIAL PLAN.

BONUS QUOTES

"LIFE IS LIKE A BANK. YOU ONLY TAKE OUT WHAT YOU PUT IN."

- WILLSTYLZNYC
C.E.O OF MAJOR RECORD LABEL

"TRUST IN GOD ALWAYS, BELIEVE IN YOURSELF ALWAYS, REMAIN HUMBLE AND NEVER LET ANYONE DEVALUE YOUR WORTH."

- DAWN ELLISON
C.E.O OF CODE 31 MEDIA

"ARTISTS NEED TO BE THEMSELVES. DON'T FOLLOW A TREND OR WHAT EVERYONE THINKS IS HOT. THAT MUSIC WAS MADE 2 TO 3 YEARS AGO. BE THE FUTURE."

- J HATCH
C.E.O. OF CREAVITE SPACE

"CONTENT, CONTENT, CONTENT. GIVE PEOPLE A REASON TO FOLLOW, ENGAGE AND BE FANS. FOR EVERY SONG YOU RELEASE, HAVE 5 TO 8 PIECES OF ARTWORK. LACK OF CONTENT WON'T BRING PEOPLE BACK TO YOUR PAGE."

- J HATCH
C.E.O. OF CREAVITE SPACE

"GET OUTSIDE, NETWORK, SHAKE HANDS, COLLABORATE AND BUILD. GET A TEAM."

- J HATCH
C.E.O. OF CREAVITE SPACE

"LEARN. EVERY DAY, LEARN FROM MISTAKES. LEARN FROM THE GREATS AS WELL AS YOUR PEERS. YOUTUBE UNIVERSITY CAN ALSO GET YOU EDUCATED BUT GET TO EVENTS, SEMINARS ETC."

- J HATCH
C.E.O. OF CREAVITE SPACE

"CREATE A 15 SECOND ELEVATOR PITCH FOR WHEN YOU MEET PEOPLE. YOU WANT THAT CONVO TO LAST SO KEEP IT SHORT AND SWEET AND IMPACTING IS KEY. ASK OPEN-ENDED QUESTIONS AND FOLLOW UP APPROPRIATELY."

- J HATCH
C.E.O. OF CREAVITE SPACE

FINAL END

CONGRATULATIONS!!! UP AND COMING ARTIST. YOU HAVE REACHED THE END OF THIS BOOK. I AM SO HONORED THAT YOU HAVE CHOSEN TO BUY AND READ THIS BOOK AND I HOPE IT HAS HELPED YOU TO OPEN UP YOUR MIND MORE AND THE MINDS OF YOUR TEAM AS WELL WHILE YOU PURSUE BECOMING THE BIGGEST ARTIST IN THE WORLD. THERE ARE GOING TO BE SMALL AND BIG OBSTACLES ON YOUR PATH. SOME OF THEM ARE GOING TO BE TERRIFYING OR EVEN POSSIBLY SEEM INSURMOUNTABLE TO THE AVERAGE ARTIST. IF YOU DON'T THINK THE MUSIC INDUSTRY LIFE IS FOR YOU, THAT'S OKAY. BUT IF YOU DO, I HOPE THIS BOOK WAS THE FIRST STEP TO OPENING UP YOUR MIND. THE LIFESTYLE OF AN UP AND COMING ARTIST IS HARD AND HAS A LOT TO DO WITH RELATIONSHIPS, BRANDING, PROMOTION, ADVERTISING AND AS MANY CATASTROPHIC FAILURES AS DAZZLING SUCCESSES. IT ALSO INVOLVES LOSSES AS WELL AS GAINS BUT FOR THOSE UP AND COMING ARTISTS WHO WANT TO CONTROL HIS OR HER OWN DESTINY, IT'S GOING TO BE WORTH IT AT THE END.

ABOUT THE AUTHOR

DJ FRANK WHYTE, AKA: FRANKLIN JONES BRIDGES, WAS BORN AND RAISED IN THE SOUTH BRONX.

I WANT TO THANK GOD FOR GIVING ME THE ABILITY TO ADD VALUE TO ALL UNSIGNED ARTISTS ON THE COME UP MINDSET. I ALSO WANT TO THANK GOD FOR GIVING ME THE STRENGTH AND KNOWLEDGE TO WRITE THIS BOOK. MY GOAL IS TO SHOW THE IMPORTANCE OF BEING IN CONTROL OF YOUR OWN DESTINY WHEN YOU STEP TOWARDS IT. NOW, AS TIME GOES ON, NEVER GIVE UP BECAUSE SUCCESS IS JUST AROUND THE CORNER AND I WILL BUILD UNSYNEDHEATTPODCAST CLUB BRICK-BY-BRICK BY USING THIS BOOK AS A MARKETING TOOL SO THAT MY PODCAST BRAND CAN GROW.

SO, WHO'S READY TO BE INTERVIEWED BY DJ FRANK WHYTE, THE HOST OF UNSYNEDHEATT PODCAST CLUB?

Made in the USA
Columbia, SC
28 August 2024

40707864R00067